Meat-Eating Plants

Meat-Eating Plants

D. M. Souza

Franklin Watts
A Division of Scholastic Inc.
New York • Toronto • London • Auckland • Sydney
Mexico City • New Delhi • Hong Kong
Danbury, Connecticut

Note to readers: Definitions for words in **bold** can be found in the Glossary at the back of this book.

Photographs ©: Dembinsky Photo Assoc.: 2 (E.R. Degginger), 52 (John Gerlach), 14, 36, 44, 45 (Bill Lea), 5 right, 19 right, 29 (Skip Moody); Dwight R. Kuhn Photography: 10, 41, 43; Peter Arnold Inc.: 24 (Fred Bavendam), 19 left (David Cavagnaro), 6 (Michael Fairchild), 5 left, 17 (Ray Pfortner), cover, 8 (Ed Reschke); Photo Researchers, NY: 27 right (Dr. Jeremy Burgess/SPL), 9 (Michael P. Gadomski), 37 (Jeff Lepore), 11 (Simon D. Pollard); Visuals Unlimited: 27 left (Cabisco), 48 (Arthur Morris), 51 (Glenn Oliver), 18, 21, 34, 50 (David Sieren), 22 (Milton H. Tierney Jr.), 31, 32 (Jerome Wexler).

The photograph on the cover shows a Venus flytrap with a true bug in its trap. The photograph opposite the title page shows a thread-leaved sundew.

Library of Congress Cataloging-in-Publication Data

Souza, D. M. (Dorothy M.)
    Meat-eating plants / D.M. Souza.
        p. cm. — (Watts Library)
    Includes bibliographical references (p.).
    ISBN 0-531-11980-7 (lib. bdg.)   0-531-16222-2 (pbk.)
    1. Carnivorous plants—Juvenile literature. [1. Carnivorous plants.] I. Title. II. Series.
QK917 .S68 2001
583'.75—dc21   2001017566

Contents

Many meat-eating plants look like alien life forms. This pitcher plant in Newfoundland, Canada, definitely grew on Earth.

Chapter One

Survival

The greenhouse is filled with hundreds of strange and beautiful plants that look as if they belong on another planet. Tips of some oddly shaped specimens barely poke out of their pots, while others rise more than 10 feet (3 meters) high, twisting and turning toward the light. The plants are in various stages of eating or digesting their dinner. A variety of insects, frogs, and perhaps a few sick birds or mice is on their menu.

The plants in this unusual greenhouse are **carnivores**, or meat eaters, and each **species** captures its meal in a unique way. First, bright colors or irresistible

Active or Passive

Carnivorous plants whose parts move in order to catch their food are said to have active traps. Those that do not move to catch food have passive traps.

scents lure creatures closer. Then sticky or slippery surfaces, downward-pointing hairs, lethal pools, or one-way entrances trap and kill the prey.

Most plants take up the water and minerals they need from the soil through their roots. Their leaves absorb carbon dioxide from the air, and, using the light of the Sun, the plants turn the water and carbon dioxide into food. This process, called **photosynthesis**, means "putting together with light."

Carnivorous plants also make food through photosynthesis. Many, however, live in wetlands called **bogs**, where water

Carnivorous plants have adapted to bogs, whose soil lacks the nutrients that plants need to grow.

Peat Bogs

Millions of years ago, during the Jurassic Period, when dinosaurs roamed swamplands, a plant called sphagnum moss flourished. Each year, some of the plants died along with other wildlife around them. The dead matter decomposed, and in the next season, new sphagnum grew on top of the old. Slowly the dead matter turned into piles and piles of **peat**. Today, some of these piles are hundreds of feet thick, and well-preserved remains of ancient humans have been uncovered in some of them. One "bog human" found in Europe is believed to be 5,300 years old.

Carnivore or Insectivore

Because some meat-eating plants eat creatures other than insects, scientists generally use the term *carnivore* rather than Charles Darwin's term *insectivore*.

carries away much of the nitrogen and other nutrients that the plants need. To obtain enough energy to grow, flower, and produce seeds for the next generation, carnivorous plants capture animals that supply the nutrients lacking in wet habitats.

Unraveling the Mystery

Nineteenth-century British naturalist Charles Darwin became so fascinated by carnivorous plants that he studied them for fifteen years. Darwin was one of the first scientists to discover that meat-eating plants produce **enzymes,** powerful chemicals that help them digest their food. His book, titled *Insectivorous Plants,* became immensely popular with the general public, and some readers traveled to distant lands in search of exotic varieties to grow in their homes or greenhouses. A few of these adventurers told of seeing tropical plants that ate humans, but these stories were merely creations of lively imaginations. No known plant has ever been capable of catching a person.

Carnivore Families

Like all living things, plants have **binomials**, scientific names consisting of two parts. The first part of a binomial gives the **genus**, or group, to which each plant belongs. The second part identifies the species, or specific kind, within the larger group. This system, first introduced in 1753 by Swedish botanist Carolus Linnaeus, makes it easier for scientists around the world to discuss individual plants that have a number of confusing local names. For example, huntsman's cups, devil's jugs, frog's breeches, and blood cups are a few of the local names of pitchers, one type of carnivorous plant.

Pitchers, which belong to the Nepenthaceae and Sarraceniaceae families, are plants with personality. Their local names include frog's breeches, blood cups, and devil's jugs.

Members of Several Carnivorous Plant Families

Family	Genus	Common Name	Number of Species	Distribution
Byblidaceae	*Byblis*	Rainbow plant	5	Australia, New Guinea
Droseraceae	*Drosera*	Sundew	141	Worldwide
	Dionaea	Venus flytrap	1	North and South Carolina
	Aldrovanda	Waterwheel	1	Europe, Africa, India, Australia
Lentibulariaceae	*Genlisea*	Corkscrew	19	South America, Africa, Madagascar
	Pinguicula	Butterwort	69	North and South America, Mexico, Europe
	Utricularia	Bladderwort	219	Worldwide
Nepenthaceae	*Nepenthes*	Tropical pitcher	60	Southeast Asia, India, Australia, Madagascar
Sarraceniaceae	*Sarracenia*	Trumpet pitcher	8	Eastern U.S., Canada
	Heliamphora	Sun pitcher	7	South America
	Darlingtonia	Cobra lily	1	California, Oregon

Plants also belong to larger groups called **families**. Members of each family might look different, but they share several characteristics in common. For example, Venus flytraps do not resemble sundews, but they are in the same family because their biological traits are similar.

Scientists have identified close to six hundred different species of carnivorous plants. Some grow on mountaintops; others live in deserts; and still others float freely beneath the surfaces of ponds. Most thrive in moist, swampy places. As new methods of identifying them are developed, plants once believed to be in one genus are sometimes found to belong in another. Also, as new meat-eating plants are discovered—or old ones disappear—the number of species changes.

In the following pages, we will spotlight a few of these unusual plants. Which is the largest, the fastest acting, and the most complex? How does each one grow, and how does it capture and digest its prey? We will also meet a handful of the plants' would-be victims and find out how some have learned to outsmart their captors.

A beetle floats helplessly in the pool of a pitcher.

Chapter Two

Slippery Slides

A beetle, following the scent of nectar, crawls up the side of a plant until it reaches an open lid lined with hundreds of soft, downward-pointing hairs. It samples the sweet nectar oozing beneath its feet and moves across what appears to be a field of honey. Once past the hairs, the beetle follows a path that leads downward inside the plant. Suddenly its legs begin to slip on the waxy surface. It turns to exit, but the hairs of the plant have become a wall of spears blocking its retreat. The beetle tumbles into a pool of murky liquid and, after a brief struggle, drowns. The soft parts of its body slowly begin to dissolve as they turn into the pitcher plant's next meal.

Many different kinds of pitcher plants grow around the world. Some lie on the ground or are only 4 inches (10 centimeters) tall. Others stand upright as high as 4 feet (120 cm). They are green, yellow, white, or various shades of red. Although pitcher plants differ in size, shape, and color, all have leaves in the form of a hollow container that holds liquid like a pitcher or vase. The liquid contains water drawn from the soil, as well as digestive acids and enzymes that the plants produce. Most creatures that fall into this pool of water become food for the plant.

American Pitchers

Spectacular stands of pitcher plants were once common in various parts of North America. The plants grew where wetlands dotted grassy and open spaces. Early European settlers were impressed by their beauty but slow to recognize their bizarre habits.

In 1700, Dr. Michel Sarrazin, a physician and botanist at the Court of Quebec, became puzzled by some local plants that were filled with the dead bodies of insects. He sent several specimens to a French scientist, who named them *Sarracenia* after Sarrazin. Later, Swedish scientist Carolus Linnaeus applied this name to all North American pitchers,

Helpers

Bacteria that live inside pitchers help to break down the bodies of insects that fall into the plants' deadly pools.

Groundwork

When lightning struck or American Indians started fires to keep bushes and trees from spreading, pitcher plants flourished in the clearings.

but not until the end of the nineteenth century did scientists begin unraveling the secrets of *Sarracenia*.

In late winter and early spring, as the weather warms, American pitcher plants start to grow from **rhizomes**, thick underground stems that store food. Most plants first produce a five-petaled flower resembling an open umbrella. Some blooms are yellow or various shades of red. The yellow ones are said to smell like cat urine.

As the flower grows, tiny leaves appear in a circular pattern at the base of the plant and slowly swell into vaselike shapes. Topping each leaf is a lid or hood that either overhangs the

Stands of pitcher plants, such as this one in California, were once common in the vast wetlands of North America.

The five-petaled flower of a trumpet pitcher

opening or grows upright. The lid is edged with sweet-smelling nectar that many insects find irresistible. Inside the lid are stiff, downward-pointing hairs that lead visitors deeper into the plant.

Covering the inside of the upper part of the pitcher is a slippery wax. Deeper inside are more downward-pointing hairs and cells with chemicals that help the plant digest its food. Each pitcher has a unique way of keeping its prey from escaping.

Yellow trumpets produce a drug that paralyzes and kills any insect that drinks their nectar. When the insects move inside the plant, they slip on the waxy surface and fall into the pool. Trumpets capture so many insects in this way that the plants sometimes topple over.

Cobra lilies have bulbous green heads with two long, red fangs hanging beneath them. When the plants sway in the breeze, they resemble snakes of the same name. Nectar is thickest on the plants' fangs, and once insects taste it and enter the plant, escape is almost impossible. Inside, the Sun shines through the hood of the plants like light through a skylight. Attracted to the light, flying insects

Its fangs swaying in the breeze, a cobra lily awaits its prey.

repeatedly bounce off the hood until they tumble into the cobra's pool and drown.

Purple pitchers grow horizontal to the ground. They have ruffled collars covered with slippery, claw-shaped hairs that drip with nectar. Insects land to sip the nectar, slip from the

Unlike its relatives, the purple pitcher's containers grow horizontal to the ground.

19

hairs, and tumble into the pitchers, from which they cannot escape.

Most pitcher leaves are active for several weeks or months before browning and dying. Then new ones grow to take their place. During winter, the plants usually shed their leaves and rest, but when spring returns, new growth appears and the insect-catching season begins once again.

Tropical Pitchers

Pitchers found mainly in the rain forests of Southeast Asia are the most spectacular carnivorous plants. They often grow as a vine running along the ground or twisting and turning in the branches of trees. These pitchers are named *Nepenthes* after an ancient drink that supposedly made the drinker forget all his troubles. Their liquid seems to have a similar effect on the organisms that drink it.

Tropical pitchers begin their growth on the ground. When they are a few months old, a vein running through the center of a leaf gradually turns into a vinelike stem called a **tendril**. The tendril lengthens, twists, and forms loops to attach itself to anything in its path as it continues reaching skyward. Some vines grow up to 50 feet (15 m) long.

Not all the plant's leaves form pitchers. In those that do, a growth appears at the tip of the tendril and slowly swells into a pitcher shape. Each variety of plant produces pitchers of different sizes and shapes. Some are small and lure tiny insects. Others are the size of footballs and can swallow prey as large as rats.

As the plant grows larger and longer, new shoots appear on the ground and eventually grow into climbing vines with more pitchers on their tips. The upper pitchers are smaller and thinner than the lower, heavier ones. Some pitchers are so different from the others that they could be mistaken for pitchers of another species.

Nepenthes ventrata, *one species of tropical pitcher. The vines that hold these pitchers grow up to 50 feet (15 m) long.*

Watery Graves

A tropical pitcher growing on Mount Kinabalu in Borneo was found to contain 4 quarts (3.8 liters) of digestive juices in its 1-foot (30-cm) container. Another held a dead rat.

Clever Invaders

While hundreds of different animals regularly disappear inside pitcher leaves, some not only avoid being caught but also snatch some of the plant's food. More than 150 animals spend at least part of their lives on or in pitcher plants. For example, some spiders spin their webs across the openings of pitcher leaves. When flying insects, attracted to the nectar of the plant, attempt to land, they are caught in the web.

A spider reaches into a pitcher to share in the plant's catch.

Some ants make their nests by drilling holes in the tendrils of tropical pitchers. The insects leave their homes and dive into the pitcher's pool. They swim around searching for large prey, such as crickets that have drowned. Several worker ants then haul the corpse up the pitcher's wall and bring it home for a feast. No one yet knows how these swimming ants manage their escape from the deadly fluid.

Mosquitoes and flies often enter a pitcher and lay their eggs in its pool. Somehow the plant's digestive juices do not harm the eggs, and after hatching, the larvae find ample food floating around them. Once they mature, they simply fly out of the plant.

The red crab spider deserves a medal for its acrobatics. It attaches itself to the inside of a pitcher leaf by a thin thread. When hungry, it lowers itself into the pool, fishes out its dinner, and shimmies back up its thread to safety.

After pitcher plants die or dry out, organisms of all kinds arrive to feed on the remaining carcasses. A few even move in or make nests out of the plants. These invaders are nature's super-recyclers.

Fish Food

In some southern states, people remove maggots from pitchers and use them as fishing bait.

Held captive by a sundew's sticky hairs, this mosquito has a grim future.

Chapter Three

Sticky Platforms

A sunlit meadow sparkles like crystals, and the smell of nectar fills the air. A mosquito circles in the air and lands on a shimmering leaf for a sip of sweet liquid. Suddenly, sensitive hairs that outnumber the tentacles of an octopus surround the mosquito. Each hair is topped with a drop of sticky liquid that holds the insect tightly in place as it tries to escape. The more it struggles, the worse its situation becomes. More hairs bend over, oozing drops of liquid onto the mosquito's body until its breathing holes are clogged. Within 15 minutes it suffocates, a victim of the innocent-looking sundew.

The scientific name for this sticky plant is *Drosera*, a Greek word that means dewy, or glistening in the Sun. More than one hundred species of sundews grow in swampy soils on every continent except Antarctica. In the deserts of western Australia, pygmy varieties are about the size of a thumbnail. They appear only during the rainy seasons and become **dormant**, or inactive, during hot summers. Other sundews are giants, with leaves that fork again and again until the plants are almost 4 feet (1 m) in diameter.

The five-petaled flowers of sundews are white, pink, orange, red, yellow, or violet. The flowers are usually small, and they bloom on tall stalks that grow well above the sticky leaves to allow pollinating insects to escape being trapped. Some species produce several dozen blooms each year.

Deadly Habits

Regardless of individual size or shape, all sundews trap their prey in the same way. Their leaves, which grow out of the ground in a circular pattern, are covered with about 250 hairs. Each hair is topped by a tiny **gland**, a cell that holds a drop of liquid as sticky as super glue. Insects are attracted to the sweet scent of the plant or its sparkling drops of liquid, and they are trapped as soon as they land.

As an insect struggles, some of the sundew's hairs bend over it or move it to the center of the leaf, where more glands can

The gland of a sundew hair

grasp it. Many sundews can curl their leaves around their prey like party favors. The king sundew of South Africa has stiff, narrow leaves 2 feet (60 cm) long. Its young leaves actually twist into knots around a victim.

Once an insect is caught, the sundew's glands begin releasing digestive enzymes that cover the helpless prey. The liquid can become so thick that it drips down the leaf as it slowly dissolves the soft parts of the insect's body. This soup is gradually absorbed by the plant. Digestion takes four to five days, depending on the size of the insect and the plant.

After it eats, the sundew releases its grip, and undigested

A sundew leaf curls firmly around a hoverfly.

27

parts either fall to the ground or are carried away by rain or breezes. Slowly, the hairs and leaves return to their upright position; fresh drops of sticky liquid reappear at the tip of each hair; and the plant awaits the arrival of its next feast. After two or three meals, individual leaves wither, but new ones soon replace them.

Few creatures are able to steal the catch of a sundew. Occasionally, a spider will spin its web from one leaf to another and try to catch an insect before it lands on a sticky platform. The spider might succeed once or twice, but eventually it moves too close to a trap and ends up becoming the sundew's next catch.

Greasy Cousins

"The little greasy one" hardly sounds like the name of a plant, but that is what the scientific name *Pinguicula* means. Butterwort is the common name of this plant, which measures

2 to 5 inches (5 to 12 cm) in diameter and is greasy to the sight and touch. There are about sixty-nine species of butterworts in the world. Mexico is home to at least forty varieties, some of which manage to grow on dry cliffs or moss-covered tree trunks.

The butterwort's trapping mechanism is similar to that of the sundew. In the spring, the plants send up white, purple, violet, or yellow flowers that look like miniature orchids. The

Drawn by sparkling lights and musty scent, insects get trapped in the greasy liquid of a butterwort.

flat green or red leaves form a circle on the ground. Each leaf is covered with thousands of tiny hairs topped with a gland that produces a drop of sticky, oily liquid. These drops glisten like those of sundews.

The butterwort's sparkling lights and musty scent lure tiny insects, such as fruit flies and gnats, onto its leaves, where they quickly become trapped. The more they struggle, the more sticky liquid flows over them. Another type of gland then releases enzymes that slowly dissolve the soft parts of the insects' bodies. Soon, a pulpy mass is ready to be absorbed.

Scientists have discovered that butterwort leaves manufacture an antibiotic that prevents microscopic fungi and bacteria from stealing undigested insects. Northern Europeans made use of this antibiotic when they rubbed butterwort leaves onto the sores of their animals to accelerate healing. While this practice might have been good for the animals, it cut short the lives of many plants.

Rainbows and Fountains

In the wilds of Australia and New Guinea grow delicate, sticky plants called *Byblis*, or rainbow plants. Their narrow stems branch again and again, sometimes trailing along the ground or climbing nearby plants. Rainbow plants sparkle in the Sun like sundews, but unlike sundews, they cannot close around their captives.

Once an insect lands on the rainbow plant, it becomes glued to sticky tentacles. The plant's glands release digestive

Even the beautiful flower of a rainbow plant glistens with drops of liquid.

Ancient Greece

In Greek mythology, Byblis was the granddaughter of Apollo. When rejected in love, she cried until she turned into a fountain. The rainbow plant was named after this mythological figure.

enzymes, and soon the food disappears. One plant can catch as many as twenty insects at the same time.

Frogs and lizards that try to steal snacks from giant rainbow plants often end up drowning in digestive juices and disintegrating. One tiny species of assassin bug has learned to outsmart the rainbow plant, however. Not only does it escape being captured, but it also sips some of the juices from the plant's victims. Scientists suspect that the bug's antics help the plant digest its meals.

This spider was looking for food when it became the victim of a Venus flytrap.

Chapter Four

Quick Triggers

A spider quickly weaves in and out of moss and bits of grass. It reaches a strange-looking plant with leaves growing in a circle close to the ground. Stepping into what looks like a miniature clamshell, it searches for food. In a fraction of a second, the shell closes over it, and the spider becomes another victim of the Venus flytrap.

In 1760, Arthur Dobbs, the British governor of North Carolina, wrote to a friend in England and described the mysterious plants that he found growing in several swampy areas. Three years later he sent a specimen to Britain, where it

The long stems, budding flowers, and leaves of a young Venus flytrap

was given the scientific name *Dionaea muscipula*, which means "mousetrap of Venus." Today, these plants are still found growing wild in the Carolinas and nowhere else.

Venus's Secret

In the springtime, five or six leaves, lying close to the earth, grow out from a rhizome like rays of light surrounding the Sun. In the center of the growth, a flower stem shoots up 12 inches (30 cm) in the air. When the stem is fully grown, small, white flowers appear.

Each leaf of the Venus flytrap has two parts: a base that widens near the top and a **lobe**, or tip, which eventually becomes the trap. As each lobe enlarges, it begins to look like a small green clam shell with tiny green teeth, called **cilia**, along one side. Gradually, the "shells" open partway to reveal two halves that are hinged along the side opposite the teeth.

36

The inner surface of each half is red, pink, or green and has three barely visible trigger hairs.

Flies and ants are lured to the flytrap by the scent of nectar flowing beneath the teeth. After it lands, the insect might wander from trap to trap, crawl over the teeth, and sip some of the nectar. Only if the fly touches two of the trigger hairs at the same time, or one trigger twice within 20 seconds, does the trap slam shut.

At first, the trap does not close tightly. Since the plant would use more energy digesting a small insect than it would gain from the nutrients, it allows some prey to escape. If an insect is large and begins to struggle, the trap closes firmly, and the teeth interlock like fingers clasped together. Glands on the inner surface of the trap begin releasing digestive juices

A flytrap's cilia close tightly around a cricket.

that eventually drown the insect, dissolve its body, and turn it into a nutritious meal. In four to ten days, the trap reopens and is ready for another catch.

Some of the Venus flytrap's leaves eventually change jobs. Instead of trapping insects, their tips remain open, and, with the help of the Sun, they make sugars. New trappers quickly grow to take their place. During winter, the plant normally enters a dormant period. Older leaves die; new traps might form, but they will not capture anything. Only when new growth appears in spring will the flesh eater's appetite return, and, if undisturbed, it can continue its carnivorous ways for many years. Some Venus flytraps live for twenty to thirty years.

Waterwheels

The waterwheel *(Aldrovanda vesiculosa)*, an amazing microscopic plant in the same family as the Venus flytrap, lives in ponds and lakes in parts of Europe, Africa, India, and Australia. This rootless mass floats freely just below the surface of the water. First described in 1699 by English botanist Leonard Plukenet, the waterwheel was officially named by Carolus Linnaeus in 1753.

Clones

The waterwheel once grew naturally in Japan but is now extinct in the wild. Botanists managed to reproduce the plant in greenhouses, and cloned *Aldrovanda* are now available.

The waterwheel's stem is 4 to 6 inches (10 to 15 cm) long. Growing around it like spokes in the hub of a wheel are groups of six to nine leaves. Each leaf ends in a miniature green trap about 0.08 inch (2 millimeters) long that, unlike the flytrap's, is closed most of the time. Guarding each trap from damage are six long, stiff hairs that surround it like a wall of swords.

When open, the waterwheel's traps await tiny swimmers such as fleas, spiders, beetles, and fish fry. After one of these animals slips inside and trips one of forty or more trigger hairs growing there, the walls of the trap slam shut around it. Miniature teeth along the edges interlock; water is squeezed out through the base; and digestive juices flood the prey. In a few hours, the waterwheel is nourished.

Each bladder of the bladderwort is about the size of a pinhead.

Chapter Five

One-Way Entrances

A copepod, a tiny relative of the shrimp, zips through a pond searching for something to eat. A faint, sweet scent draws it toward a feathery plant floating nearby. In the next instant, a soft swooshing is heard as the copepod is trapped inside what looks like a tiny plastic bag. The bladderwort, one of the strangest, most complex carnivorous plants, has just caught its prey.

Bladderworts (*Utricularia*) can be found on almost every continent. Various species float in ponds or bogs. Others grow under damp, sandy soil or in swamplands. Some bladderworts are **epiphytes** that hide in the wet, rotten bark of trees. Like other epiphytes, they do not harm the tree but use it for support. A few bladderworts even grow on rocks under waterfalls. These and other rock-clinging plants are known as **lithophytes**.

Bladderworts consist of thin, rootless, creeping or floating stems with feathery branches. Many are 3 feet (1 m) long. Growing from the stems are hundreds, sometimes thousands, of **bladders**, or clear hollow bags, which are about the size of a pinhead. Although small, each trap is swift and precise when catching prey.

In 1875, German botanist Ferdinand Cohn was studying some bladderworts that he kept in an aquarium. One day he dropped water fleas into the tank to see what would happen. He noticed nothing unusual, but the next day, when he inspected the tank, all the insects had disappeared. Searching closely, he spotted them inside the now-inflated bladders.

Bladderworts in Action

When examined under a microscope, the bladderwort reveals its inner workings. Each bladder has an opening covered by a hinged door at one end. Long hairs surrounding this opening

The tiny container of a bladderwort encloses its prey.

guide prey closer to where the plant can reach it. At the base of the entrance are four bristles that point outward. As soon as a small organism, such as a water flea, trips one of these bristles, the door swings inward, pulling the flea like a vacuum cleaner. The door slams shut, excess water is pumped out, and a sticky liquid tightly seals the entrance. The entire action takes about as long as the blink of an eye.

Digestive juices slowly begin working, and in 15 minutes to 2 hours (depending on the size of the catch), the plant has finished eating. The trap is reset and awaits its next tidbit. One bladder can catch as many as fifteen small animals during its life span.

In addition to copepods, water fleas, and microscopic organisms, a bladder occasionally catches larger meals. In this case it must take repeated gulps, holding its catch tightly until it resets its trap and floods its meal with digestive juices again and again.

If it were not for a rainbow of flowers appearing in spring, bladderworts might go unnoticed or be mistaken for weeds.

Blooming bladderworts decorate a swamp in South Carolina. Without its distinctive flowers, the plant would probably go unnoticed.

The blooms, which can be as small as grains of rice or as large as plums, are prized for their beauty. When the delicate yellow, pink, purple, violet, red, or multicolored flowers first appear, they give no hint of the deadly habits of the feathery branches beneath them.

The Corkscrew

The corkscrew plant *(Genlisea)* grows in parts of South America, Africa, and Madagascar, in many of the same moist locations as bladderworts. It looks and acts like no other carnivorous plant. Small, spoon- or strap-shaped leaves lie flat on the ground in a circular pattern, and numerous tube-shaped stalks spread out underground or underwater. Partway down each stalk is a hollow sac that acts as the plant's stomach. As a stalk grows downward, it branches into an upside-down Y. A slit or opening forms on each part of the Y and spirals around it like a corkscrew.

When small creatures swim close to *Genlisea* and slip inside its openings, there is no exiting. They find themselves in a tunnel lined with bristly hairs that force them to travel in only one direction. After they reach the plant's stomach, digestive juices begin to slowly dissolve their bodies.

Darwin was the first scientist to suspect that corkscrew plants are carnivorous, but he was unable to figure out what they eat. In 1998, Wilhelm Barthlott and several other German botanists performed experiments in an effort to solve the mystery. Knowing that corkscrews grow in areas with few

Double Jeopardy

Some species of *Genlisea* are believed to produce two types of traps: small ones close to the surface and larger ones deeper in wet soil.

insects, the scientists placed a number of one-celled animals called **protozoans** near a plant. The tiny organisms were immediately drawn inside the slits as if pulled by magnets.

Genlisea, the scientists discovered, sends out chemicals to lure protozoans, which swim closer and are quickly swallowed. The corkscrew is the only carnivorous variety known to specialize in protozoans. After more than one hundred years of research, the question that puzzled Darwin was finally answered.

Humans are the main predators of carnivorous plants and their habitats. Here, a ditch-digging machine drains marshland in New Jersey.

Chapter Six

Meat Eaters in Danger

Carnivorous plants are able to do what no other plants can—capture, kill, and digest other organisms. Many produce rare, beautiful flowers and leaves. Unfortunately, the plants' uniqueness has worked against them. Meat-eating plants have become prized possessions of larger, more powerful **predators**: humans.

Dealers, anxious to make a profit, collect carnivorous plants in the wild. They repeatedly remove them from certain areas until none remain, or they handle

The unusual leaves of this white trumpet pitcher might end up in a vase on someone's dining-room table.

them so carelessly that the plants die. To meet the demand for the strange and beautiful leaves of certain North American pitchers, florists turn to suppliers who remove the plants' flowers. Since each bloom contains the seeds for the next generation, this practice threatens the existence of pitchers in the wild.

Environmental changes also endanger the carnivores. When bogs and swamps are drained and filled to make room for housing, roads, office complexes, and shopping malls, the species that grew in those areas disappear forever. In the United States, only 3 to 5 percent of the wetlands remain where these plants once thrived. In the tropics, as areas are burned and converted into farmlands, many exotic carnivores are also destroyed.

Peat and sphagnum, substances found where meat-eating plants grow, are increasingly in demand as soil conditioners by

A crane clears Alaska wetlands to make way for a new road.

Nonprofit organizations work hard to preserve wetlands and the meat-eating plants that thrive in them.

52

home gardeners and landscapers. When these products are harvested for commercial use, the bogs and their contents are damaged. Commercial harvesters in Britain have already removed more than 90 percent of the country's peat.

Several organizations work to save carnivorous plants and their wetlands. The Nature Conservancy, a nonprofit group based in Arlington, Virginia, purchases endangered habitats so that their species can be saved. The Convention on International Trade of Endangered Species (CITES) is another organization trying to preserve wild species. Member nations around the globe set up rules and regulations to protect threatened and endangered species from being collected in one country and shipped to another.

Today, state and federal governments impose stiff fines on anyone found collecting endangered carnivorous plants in their native habitats. In North Carolina, for example, a first offense can cost from $100 to $500. A second offense results in a fine of up to $2,000.

You, too, can help by learning more about wetlands and by trying to protect and preserve the plants that grow there. Let others know about these fascinating plants and the threats to their existence. Only with the help of some friends will the meat-eating plants survive.

Threats to Flytraps

Before CITES was established, an estimated 250,000 Venus flytraps were illegally removed from the Carolinas and shipped overseas.

Glossary

binomial—a two-part scientific name that includes the genus and species of an organism

bladder—a sac that holds liquid or gas in an organism

bog—an area of wet, spongy soil that is low in nutrients

carnivore—a meat-eating organism

cilia—small, hairlike structures

dormant—inactive

enzyme—a protein that triggers chemical reactions, such as those involved in digestion, in living cells

epiphyte—a plant that grows on or in another plant for the purpose of support

family—a major category in the classification of plants and animals

genus—a group of closely related species

gland—a cell or organ that holds fluid

lithophyte—a plant that grows on rocks

lobe—a curved or rounded tip that projects from another body, as the lobe of a human ear or the trap of a Venus flytrap

peat—an organic material found in moist, swampy areas

photosynthesis—the process by which plants change water and carbon dioxide into food

predator—a plant or animal that captures and eats another

protozoan—a one-celled organism, such as an amoeba, belonging to the phylum Protozoa

rhizome—a thick plant stem that grows just under the surface of the ground

species—a group of closely related organisms

tendril—a curly, threadlike offshoot, as in the tendril of a tropical pitcher plant

To Find
Out More

Books

Aaseng, Nathan. *Meat-Eating Plants.* Berkeley Heights, NJ: Enslow Publications, 1996.

Gentle, Victor. *Pitcher Plants: Slippery Pits of No Escape.* Milwaukee: Gareth Stevens Publishing, 1996.

Lecoufle, Marcel. *Carnivorous Plants.* New York: Sterling Publishing Co., 1990.

Overbeck, Cynthia. *Carnivorous Plants.* Minneapolis, MN: Lerner Publications, 1982.

Wexler, Jerome. *Secrets of the Venus Flytrap.* New York: Dodd Mead, 1981.

Videos and Images Online

Carnivorous Plants. Baker & Taylor Video, 1990.

Death Trap. Time-Life Video, 1989.

http://www.sarracenia.com/faq.html
This site has images and answers to frequently asked questions about carnivorous plants.

Organizations and Online Sites

International Carnivorous Plant Society
P.O. Box 330
3310 East Yorba Linda Blvd.
Fullerton, CA 92831-1709
http://www.carnivorousplants.org
This organization publishes a quarterly magazine packed with photos and information about meat-eating plants.

Meadowview Biological Research Station
8390 Fredericksburg Turnpike
Woodford, VA 22580
http://www.pitcherplant.org/
This organization is dedicated to preserving and restoring pitcher-plant bogs on the coastal plains of Maryland and Virginia.

The Nature Conservancy
4245 North Fairfax Drive, Suite 100
Arlington, VA 22203-1606
http://www.tnc.org
This nonprofit group purchases and manages endangered habitats.

A Note on Sources

Several years ago I visited California Carnivores, an indoor garden where five hundred varieties of meat-eating plants from around the world grow under one roof. Owned by Peter D'Amato, it holds the largest collection of carnivorous plants in the world.

After touring this fascinating place, I was hooked on the plants, and I purchased a Venus flytrap and a sundew to watch in action. D'Amato's book, *The Savage Garden*, provided tips on caring for my plant pets, as well as information on other "savages."

Watching the plants catch their meals taught me many things, but I wanted to learn more. A reference librarian directed me to several excellent sources, including Donald E. Schnell's *Carnivorous Plants of the United States and Canada* and Adrian Slack's *Carnivorous Plants*. Magazine articles and Web sites offered images, more current information, and additional references, such as Allen Lowrie's *Carnivorous Plants of Australia, Vols. 2 and 3*, and Tony Camilleri's *Carnivorous Plants.*

I also discovered the International Carnivorous Plant Society, which publishes a colorful quarterly newsletter packed with current findings by scientists, details on newly discovered species, photos, plants, and books for sale—everything anyone interested in the meat eaters might wish to know. I was now on my way to building my own collection of these amazing plants and sharing what I had learned with others.

Special thanks go to this book's two content consultants: Dr. Barry Meyers-Rice, biologist and editor, and Jerrold I. Davis, Department of Plant Biology, Cornell University.

—*D. M. Souza*

Index

Numbers in *italics* indicate illustrations.

About the Author

After teaching in both middle grades and high school for several years, D. M. Souza began freelance writing. She especially enjoys writing about science topics and, in her free time, often tracks and studies the wildlife living around her solar-powered mountain cabin in Northern California. Souza has written more than two dozen books for young people, including *Freaky Flowers* and *What Is a Fungus?* for Franklin Watts.